Intonation in Context
Student's Book

Intonation in Context

Intonation practice for
upper-intermediate and
advanced learners of English

Student's Book

Barbara Bradford

Advisory Editor: David Brazil

CAMBRIDGE
UNIVERSITY PRESS

Published by the Press Syndicate of the University of Cambridge
The Pitt Building, Trumpington Street, Cambridge CB2 1RP
40 West 20th Street, NY 10011–4211 USA
10 Stamford Road, Oakleigh, Victoria 3166, Australia

© Cambridge University Press 1988

First published 1988
Fourth printing 1992

Printed and bound in Great Britain by
J. W. Arrowsmith Ltd, Bristol

ISBN 0 521 31914 5 Student's Book
ISBN 0 521 31915 3 Teacher's Book
ISBN 0 521 26490 1 Cassette

CE

Contents

Acknowledgements

I should like to thank:

– David Brazil, my advisory editor, whose work at Birmingham University inspired the development of this material. It has been necessary, however, to simplify his description of the system of intonation and to make some adaptations in presenting it here for teaching purposes. I take full responsibility for these simplifications and adaptations.

– The many students who have worked with the material in its various stages of development.

– The teachers and institutions who worked with the pilot edition and whose comments were so valuable in the production of the final edition.

– Studio AVP for producing the recordings, which are central to the course.

– The Phonetics Department at the School of Oriental and African Studies, London University, for assistance in obtaining the intonation contour displays.

– My family and close friends for their support and enthusiasm throughout.

– Finally, my editors, Christine Cairns and Jeanne McCarten, and Alison Silver, who edited the typescript.

BB

Cartoons by Tony Hall
Drawings by Leslie Marshall and Chris Evans
Book design by Peter Ducker MSTD

Introduction

This introduction tells you about the aims and approach of this course and how to use it.

The title

It is always a good idea to look carefully at the title of a book or article because it can tell you a lot about the content and prepare you for the approach which is taken. So, in this case, what is 'intonation' and what is meant here by 'context'?

Intonation is a feature of the spoken language. It consists of the continuous changing of the pitch of a speaker's voice to express meanings. You will have realised that people can mean different things by using the same group of words, arranged in the same order, but saying them in different ways. Here are two diagrams (fundamental frequency traces) which show the same group of words spoken in two different ways. The pitch rises and falls in different places.

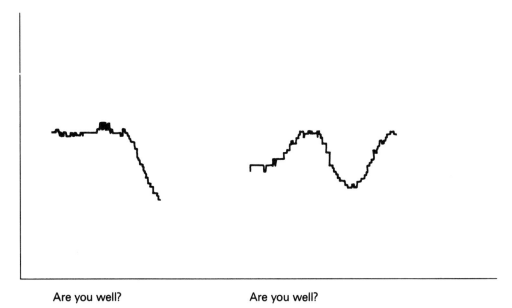

Are you well?　　　　　　　　Are you well?

A speaker is able to make the group of words mean what he/she wants it to mean by choosing the right intonation.

Context means the situation in which things are said. Features of the situation include the place and time, but also the roles the speakers are playing, their relationship, the knowledge and experience they already share and what has already been said. Speakers are influenced by all of these things when they choose the intonation of what they say.

Who is the course for?

Intonation in Context is for upper-intermediate and advanced students of English who would like to improve their listening and speaking skills.

It has been designed for students working in a class with a teacher, but it is also suitable for individual students working privately.

The work in the course centres on listening and speaking activities so you will need to be able to use listening/recording facilities. The cassette is therefore an essential part of the course. You may find it useful to record your own voice when doing the activities and to be able to compare your responses with the recorded models.

The aims

The course has two main aims:
i) to make you more sensitive to intonation so that you have a better understanding of the English you hear;
ii) to help you express yourself more fluently and precisely in English, and with greater confidence.

The approach

This course does not try to relate intonation to grammar or to mood or attitudes. Instead, it presents intonation as a *system* which you can learn and put to use to convey *meanings*. The choices from the system which enable speakers to convey their intended meanings depend on the features of the context.

To be able to use the system you will need to learn about its separate features. These are introduced one at a time in this course. In each of six units you will focus on one feature and the choices which can be made from that part of the system. The other two units revise and practise what you have learnt.

To learn any system we need special terms by which we can refer to its parts. Therefore, as you work through this course and learn the system, you may find that some terms are new to you. Each one will be fully described and explained in context. However, some important terms are included in the glossary on page 61. You may find it useful to become familiar with them before you begin.

The organisation of the course

There are eight units in the course. You should work through them in the order in which they are presented to build up the system of intonation. You may wish to return to some parts to revise, but work through the units from 1 to 8 to begin with.

Units 1, 2, 3, 5, 6, and 7 follow a regular pattern:

1 Sensitisation

One feature of English intonation is demonstrated to help you to become aware of the choices a speaker can make and how they sound. There is usually a conversation for listening, with questions to familiarise you with the content and the context. Then you will listen to an extract from the conversation which is accompanied by tasks which focus your attention on the particular feature.

2 Explanation

Here the feature is described and the meanings of the choices a speaker can make are explained. These are always shown to relate to the context. Any special transcription is introduced in this section.

3 Imitation

You are given opportunities to practise the feature of intonation by repeating extracts from the conversation you have heard in the Sensitisation section.

4 Practice activities

There is a variety of activities: some will help you to recognise the feature and some give you practice in producing it – in context.

5 Communication activity

This activity requires you to work with a partner and exchange information. It gives you the opportunity to think about the feature you have been learning about and to use it in a freer situation. (This section is not relevant for students working alone.)

Units 4 and 8 are for revision and practice of the features you have learnt in the preceding units. They do not follow the set pattern, but include a variety of the kinds of activities you have worked on in the other units.

Assessing your progress

Throughout the course try to make yourself aware of what you are doing when you speak and be self-critical. Listen carefully as you compare your responses with the model responses on the cassettes. If you are working with other students, invite criticism from them, and be prepared to help them in the same way.

You may feel at the end of the course that you have made more progress in hearing and understanding the intonation of other speakers than you have made in using it yourself. This is natural. Remember, you were able to understand your native language before you were able to use it effectively to express yourself. This course is only a beginning. It will give you initial training, and when you are aware of intonation as a system you will be able to continue practising all the time you are speaking English.

I hope you find the course interesting and that you will continue to improve in your use of intonation long after you have finished it.

NOTE

Students working without a teacher will need to have the Teacher's Book, which contains the answers to the exercises, the tapescripts and further explanatory notes.

Barbara Bradford

Unit 1   Highlighting

In any conversation between speakers of English some words are more noticeable than others. We can say the speakers *highlight* these words.

1   Sensitisation

1.1 Listen to this conversation and try to answer the questions.

i)   What is Alan trying to do?
ii) Why does he find it so difficult?
iii) How does Louise react to his attempts?

1.2 Now listen to this short extract from the conversation. In the transcript below draw a box round the words which you think are most noticeable.

Alan: Turn slightly towards me.
              Your head slightly towards me.
Louise: Right?
Alan: No – only slightly towards me.

Compare your transcript with a partner. Try to say why the same word is sometimes highlighted and sometimes not.

1.3 Listen to the conversation again. Listen for more examples (find at least three) where a word which occurs more than once is sometimes highlighted and sometimes not.

2 Explanation

2.1 A speaker highlights the words which are most significant at that point in the conversation.

e.g. ⬚Turn⬚ slightly ⬚towards⬚ me.

Alan could have asked Louise to move in several different ways. For example, he could have said any of these:

walk		to the right
come	slightly	to the left
turn		towards me

At this point in the conversation Alan wants Louise to notice:
a) turn – this is the action he wants her to take.
b) towards – she doesn't know which way he wants her to turn.
So, at this point he highlights 'turn' and 'towards'.

Later, he repeats the two words 'slightly towards' but this time he highlights 'slightly' because this is the one she hasn't responded to:

No – only ⬚slightly⬚ towards me.

A word may at one point in the conversation be very significant and at another point be part of the background of what the speaker says. In order to make the hearer notice the word when it is significant the speaker highlights it.

2.2 A highlighted word is more noticeable because it contains a prominent syllable. One important feature of a syllable which is heard as prominent is a slightly raised pitch. It may also be louder, but this is not the most important feature.

2.3 When we wish to show which syllables are prominent we print them in small CAPITAL letters:

e.g. TURN slightly toWARDS me.
Your HEAD slightly towards me.

3 Imitation

3.1 Listen again to these extracts and repeat each one.

Alan: TURN slightly toWARDS me
Your HEAD slightly towards me
Only SLIGHTly towards me

3.2 Now try these. Listen first and then repeat each one.

i) JUST a bit further to the RIGHT
I mean to MY right

ii) LIKE THAT
NOT QUITE like that

iii) HOW about a SMILE
CAN you make it a more NATural smile

4 Practice activities

4.1 Listen to the following utterances: you will hear each one twice. Decide which of the questions, (a) or (b), provides a suitable context for what you hear. The highlighting is not transcribed here, so you must recognise which word is made prominent.

i) They hired a car.
a) Did they take the car?
b) Did they hire bikes?

ii) No, the train was delayed.
a) Had she already arrived at the station?
b) Was the plane late?

iii) The bank's on the corner.
a) Where's the bank?
b) What's on the corner?

iv) I sent him a letter.
a) Aren't you going to send Tony a letter?
b) How does Mr Pringle know your news?

v) It's next Tuesday.
   a) Is it your birthday next week?
   b) Was it your birthday last Tuesday?

4.2 First listen to this short conversation. Then listen again and repeat B's part.

A: What did you have for starters?
B: I had chicken soup.
A: And what did the others have?
B: Chris had tomato soup and James had tomato salad.

Now go on. Take B's part and respond to A's questions. Or work with a partner and take it in turns to take the parts of A and B. Highlight the words you want to make most noticeable in each of the responses.

i)   A: And what did you have for dessert?
    B: I had apple pie.
    A: What did the others have?
    B: Chris had cherry pie and James had cherry cake.

ii) A: It's your birthday this month, isn't it?
    B: Yes. It's the thirty-first.
    A: Are both your sisters' birthdays this month too?
    B: Yes. Sarah's is the twenty-first and Jenny's is the twenty-fourth.

iii) A: Where did he wait for you?
    B: At the back entrance.
    A: And where had you arranged to meet?
    B: At the main entrance, which is right on the main street.

iv) A: When did you visit Japan?
    B: I went last year.
    A: And are you going again?
    B: Yes. I'm going again this year. In fact, I'm going this month.

v)   A: What's the problem?
    B: She's got black shoes.
    A: And why is that a problem?
    B: She needed white shoes to go with her white dress.

4.3 Listen to this example. The same or similar words are used to reply to three different questions.

A: Is Colin happy in his job?
B: NO. He's GOING to MOVE.

A: What's Colin going to do?
B: He's going to MOVE.

A: Did you say Colin had moved?
B: No. He's GOING to move.

Now go on. Take B's part and use the same words to give suitable answers to the three questions.

i) A: When is Peter's birthday?
   A: Is Peter's birthday the thirty-first?
   A: Did you say Peter's birthday was the twenty-fourth?

   B: (No.) It's the twenty-first.

ii) A: Are you going to the concert tonight?
    A: How will you get in?
    A: Do you think there'll be any tickets left?

    B: I've got a ticket.

iii) A: What does Ann do?
     A: Does Ann sell books?
     A: Did you say Ann makes clothes?

     B: (No.) She sells clothes.

iv) A: What's the matter with Charles?
    A: Is he afraid he'll catch a cold?
    A: Has Charles got flu?

    B: (No.) He's got a cold.

v) A: When are you leaving?
   A: Shall we see you here on Thursday morning?
   A: You'll miss the party on Wednesday night, won't you?

   B: (Yes.) (No.) We're not going till Thursday night.

4.4 For this activity work with a partner if possible. B uses the same words to respond to the two different things that A says.

i) A: Paul looks happy!
   A: I think Paul needs a new car.

   B: He's got a new car.

ii) A: We must get some flowers.
    A: Don't forget to get them a present.

    B: I've got some flowers.

iii) A: Let's go to Paris.
     A: Have you had a good weekend?

     B: I've been to Paris.

iv) A: You need something hot.
A: The soup's good here.

B: Then I'll have some soup.

v) A: How did you know it was Mike who rang?
A: Why hasn't he written?

B: He said he'd phone.

5 Communication activity

Student A – look at activity 1 for the information you need.
Student B – look at activity 5 for your information.

Unit 2   Telling and referring

As they are speaking, speakers of English make the pitch of their voices rise and fall in a way which has meaning for their hearers. We call these pitch movements *tones*.

1   Sensitisation

1.1 Listen to this part of a conversation.

Dave: What shall we give Claire?
Gill: Well, as she likes reading, we could give her a book.

1.2 Listen again to what Dave says:

Dave: What shall we give Claire?

i)   Can you say in which direction the pitch of Dave's voice moves on 'give Claire'?
ii) Do you think they have just been talking about Claire?
iii) Do you think they have already spoken about giving Claire something?

1.3 Now listen again to what Gill says:

Gill: Well, as she likes reading, we could give her a book.

i)   Can you say in which direction the pitch of Gill's voice moves on 'reading' and on 'book'?
ii) Does Gill assume that Dave knows Claire likes reading?

2   Explanation

There are two main kinds of tone in English: those which finally rise (↗ and ∨↗), and those which finally fall (↘ and ∧↘). Of these, the two which seem to occur most frequently are the ∨↗ and the ↘. We shall concentrate on these two tones in this and the next unit.

The tones

i)   THE FALL (↘)

Speakers use falling tones in parts of utterances which contain information they think is new for their hearers – when they are *telling* them something they don't already know. It may be information in response to a question, e.g. Gill: ... we could give her a book.

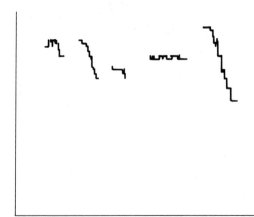

we could give her a book

Or it may be information the speakers present as new, something they want their hearers to know about or consider, e.g. Dave: What shall we give Claire?

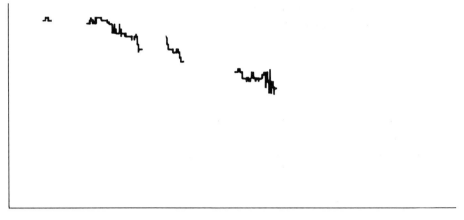

What shall we give Claire?

ii) THE FALL-RISE ($\vee$)

Speakers use fall-rise tones in parts of utterances which contain ideas they think their hearers already know about or have experience of. They *refer* to something shared by themselves and the hearers at that point in the conversation. It may be something they both know about, e.g. Gill: Well, as she likes reading ... Or it may be something which has just been stated or implied in the conversation.

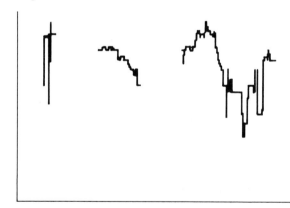

as she likes reading

Tone units and tonic syllables

When we want to describe intonation we need to divide the natural flow of speech into *tone units*. Each tone unit contains one *tonic syllable*. This is a prominent syllable on which a pitch movement begins. The tonic syllable is always the last prominent syllable in a tone unit.

The transcription

We show these features by using:
i)   Small CAPITAL letters for prominent syllables.
ii) UNDERLINING for tonic syllables.
iii) Two slanting lines (//) to mark the beginnings and ends of tone units.
iv) An arrow (↘) or (↗) to indicate the tone which begins on the next tonic syllable.
     e.g. // ↗ as she likes READing //

3 Imitation

3.1 First listen to these two examples of the falling tone from the conversation. The pitch begins to fall on the tonic syllable.

↘ What shall we GIVE Claire?

↘ we could give her a BOOK

Now listen again and repeat each utterance. The arrows remind you to make the pitch of your voice begin to fall on the tonic syllable.

3.2 Listen to this example of the fall-rise tone from the conversation. The fall-rise movement begins on the tonic syllable and the pitch of the voice continues to rise.

↗ as she likes READing

Listen again and this time repeat the utterance. The arrow reminds you to start the fall-rise movement of pitch on the tonic syllable.

3.3 Now listen to this utterance which contains both a falling and a fall-rise tone. Listen the first time, and then listen and repeat.

↗ as she likes READing ↘ we could give her a BOOK

4 Practice activities

4.1 Listen to this example:

B: // ↘ I've got some LETTers to write // ↗ on TUESday //

This is a suitable response in a context like this:

A: How about coming out for a drink on Tuesday?
B: // ↗ Un<u>FOR</u>tunately // ↘ I've got some <u>LETT</u>ers to write // ↗ on <u>TUES</u>day //

where Tuesday is an idea already shared by A and B.

Now go on in the same way.
A is trying to persuade B to go out for a drink but B has something arranged every night and can't accept. Some ideas are given to help B give reasons for being unavailable, but you may think of your own.

i) A: Why don't we go on Wednesday then?
    B: // ↗ I'm a<u>FRAID</u> // ↘ (meeting) // ↗ on <u>WED</u>nesday //

ii) A: Can you go on Thursday?
    B: // ↗ <u>SO</u>rry // ↘ (homework) // ↗ on <u>THURS</u>day //

iii) A: Well, let's go on Friday, after work.
     B: // ↘ I <u>CAN'T</u> // ↘ (phone call) // ↗ on <u>FRI</u>day //

iv) A: Could you manage Saturday, then?
    B: // ↘ I'm afraid <u>NOT</u> // ↘ (theatre) // ↗ on <u>SAT</u>urday //

v) A: Oh dear. Sunday perhaps?
    B: // ↘ It's im<u>POSS</u>ible // ↘ (visit/sister) // ↗ on <u>SUN</u>day //

vi) A: Well, that just leaves Monday ...
    B: // ↗ <u>SO</u>rry // ↘ (things to do) // ↗ on <u>MON</u>day //
    I need some time for myself!

4.2 Listen to this example:

B: // ↗ I'm <u>GO</u>ing to the <u>THE</u>atre // ↘ on <u>SAT</u>urday //

This is a suitable response in a context like this:

A: Let's go to the theatre.
B: // ↗ I'm <u>GO</u>ing to the <u>THE</u>atre // ↘ on <u>SAT</u>urday //

where the theatre is an idea already shared by A and B.

Now go on in the same way. A and B have finally arranged to meet. But they haven't decided what to do. Whatever A suggests B has either done already or is going to do it soon.

i) A: Let's go to the sports centre, then.
    B: // ↗   // ↘ to<u>MORR</u>ow //

ii) A: Would you like to see a film?
    B: // ↗   // ↘ this <u>EVE</u>ning //

iii) A: Shall we visit Janet? She keeps inviting us.
    B: // ∨↗   // ↘ next <u>MON</u>day //

iv) A: We could try the new Italian restaurant.
    B: // ∨↗   // ↘ last <u>SAT</u>urday //

v) A: Why don't we drive to the coast?
    B: // ∨↗   // ↘ on <u>THURS</u>day //

vi) A: Well, let's just stay in and listen to some music.
    B: // ∨↗   // ↘ <u>LAST</u> night //
    That's what we always do in the end!

4.3 Listen to the following utterances, which you will hear twice. In each case mark the tones in the transcript and decide which of the questions, (a) or (b), provides a suitable context for what you hear.

i)   //   I met <u>RO</u>Bert //   this <u>MORN</u>ing //
   a) Who did you meet today?
   b) When did you meet Robert?

ii)   //   He <u>TOLD</u> me //   he was in <u>LOVE</u> //
   a) What did he tell you?
   b) How do you know he's in love?

iii)   //   She's started to <u>WOR</u>RY //   about her e<u>XAMS</u> //
   a) How does Sue feel about her exams?
   b) What is Sue worrying about?

iv)   //   I learned <u>SPAN</u>ish //   at <u>SCHOOL</u> //
   a) Where did you learn to speak Spanish?
   b) Did you learn any languages at school?

4.4 In this example the same words are used as responses in two different contexts. First listen, and then practise making the responses in the two different ways.

A: There's a very good fish restaurant where we could have dinner tonight.
B: // ∨↗ I had <u>FISH</u> // ↘ for <u>LUNCH</u> //

A: We won't have time to eat later. So I hope you've had something already.
B: // ↘ I had <u>FISH</u> // ∨↗ for <u>LUNCH</u> //

Now go on. Use the same words to make suitable responses in the two different contexts.

i)   A: My cousin's coming to stay in April. I'd like you to meet him.
   A: So – you're going to France and Italy for your holidays next year. Paris is lovely in May and June.

   B: //   I'm going to <u>FRANCE</u> //   in <u>AP</u>ril //

ii) A: I always meet John when I go to the swimming pool. He must go there every day I think.

   A: I don't know how Alan is going to keep in shape, working such long hours at the office.

   B: //   He's taken up <u>SWIMM</u>ing //   to keep <u>FIT</u> //

iii) A: I think I should write to the managing director but I don't know where to send the letter.

   A: I complained to the shop in the High Street but the letter I got in reply came from London.

   B: //   The firm's head <u>OFF</u>ice //   is in <u>LON</u>don //

iv) A: His exam results were good. What did he do when he got them?

   A: So, he's hoping to go to university. Has he applied yet?

   B: //   He app<u>LIED</u> for uni<u>VER</u>sity //   when he <u>KNEW</u> he had <u>PASSED</u> //

5 Communication activity

Student A – look at activity 4 for the information you need.
Student B – look at activity 8 for your information.

Unit 3   More telling and referring

In Unit 2 we looked at the two main tones in English: the fall ($\searrow$) and the fall-rise ($\vee$). In this unit we concentrate on these same tones and practise using them in longer pieces of conversation.

1   Sensitisation

1.1 Listen to this first part of a conversation.

Lisa: Hello, Tony. Did you go for your interview yesterday?
Tony: Hi, Lisa. Yes, I did.
Lisa: How did it go?
Tony: All right, I think.
Lisa: All right? You don't sound very sure.

1.2 Now listen to the same part of the conversation again.

   i)   In the transcript below try to identify the tones which are not marked.

> Lisa: . . . HELLO <u>TON</u>y //   DID you go for your <u>IN</u>terview yesterday //
> Tony: // ↘ <u>HI</u> Lisa //   <u>YES</u> //   I <u>DID</u> //
> Lisa: //   HOW did it <u>GO</u> //
> Tony: // ↘ All <u>RIGHT</u> // ✓ I <u>THINK</u> //
> Lisa: //   All <u>RIGHT</u> //   You <u>DON'T</u> sound very <u>SURE</u> //

   ii) Can you explain why Lisa or Tony has chosen to use a telling (↘) tone or a referring (✓) tone in each case you have marked?

2 Explanation

Speakers choose falling (↘) tones when they think that what they say will increase their hearer's knowledge.

   In Unit 2 we said that speakers choose fall-rise (✓) tones when they are referring to something already stated or implied in the conversation. It is not always easy to identify anything in the immediate context. What speakers say in this tone refers to something they know or assume is already known to both the hearers and themselves.

   So speakers may use fall-rise tones to refer, not to something which has been said, but to something which is part of the background knowledge or experience they share with their hearers.

In the conversation you heard three ways in which the referring tone functions:

i)   To refer to something already stated,
    e.g. Lisa: // ✓ All <u>RIGHT</u> //

ii) To check something is as it is assumed,
    e.g. // ✓ DID you go for your <u>IN</u>terview yesterday //

iii) To refer to something which is or has become part of their common background knowledge/experience,
    e.g. // ✓ You <u>DON'T</u> sound very <u>SURE</u> //

3 Imitation

3.1 Listen again to this part of the conversation where Lisa refers to what Tony has already stated.

> Tony: // ↘ All <u>RIGHT</u> // ✓ I <u>THINK</u> //
> Lisa: // ✓ All <u>RIGHT</u> //

Listen again and repeat both parts.

3.2 Listen to this part of the conversation in which Lisa checks that what she presumes is, in fact, true.

Lisa: // ↗ DID you go for your INterview yesterday //
Tony: // ↘ HI Lisa // ↘ YES // ↘ I DID //
Lisa: // ↘ HOW did it GO //

Listen again and repeat Lisa's part.

3.3 Listen to this utterance from the conversation in which Lisa refers to something which at that point has become part of their common knowledge.

Lisa: // ↗ You DON'T sound very SURE //

Listen again and repeat, this time including the previous tone unit.

Lisa: // ↗ All RIGHT // ↗ You DON'T sound very SURE //

4 Practice activities

4.1 You have already practised this part of the conversation in which Lisa checks what she presumes is true.

Lisa: // ↗ DID you go for your INterview yesterday //
Tony: // ↘ HI Lisa // ↘ YES // ↘ I DID //
Lisa: // ↘ HOW did it GO //

The following short dialogues are similar. In each case A chooses a ↗ tone to check something, and then chooses a ↘ tone to continue. Practise reading the dialogues before listening to the recording.

i) A: // ↗ Is that the poLICE station //
    B: // ↘ YES madam //
    A: // ↘ I WANT to report a ROBBery //

ii) A: // ↗ Are these EATing apples //
     B: // ↘ YES // ↘ they're FRENCH //
     A: // ↘ I'd like a KIlo please //

iii) A: // ↗ Did you hear the NEWS this morning //
     B: // ↘ YES // ↘ I DID //
     A: // ↘ What do you THINK about it //

iv) A: // ↗ Have you been to the exhiBItion //
     B: // ↘ YES // ↘ I HAVE //
     A: // ↘ Isn't it INteresting //

v)   A: // ↗ DID you hear what she just SAID //
     B: // ↘ I DID //
     A: // ↘ That's really inCREDible //

4.2 Listen to this example. B's reply is so general that it does not tell A anything which extends A's knowledge, and so he uses a ∨↗ tone.

A: // ∨↗ Is he DOing his ESSay //
B: // ∨↗ He's WRITing SOMEthing //

This sort of reply is often used as a way of avoiding answering a question.

Now go on. Practise the conversations in pairs before listening to the recording.
 You may be able to think of other replies to A's questions, said with the same intonation.

i) A: // ∨↗ HAVE you had DINNer //
    B: // ∨↗ I've had SOMEthing //

ii) A: // ↘ Has he SENT the LETTer //
    B: // ∨↗ He was GOing to //

iii) A: // ↘WHEN will it START //
    B: // ∨↗ It SHOULDn't be LONG now //

iv) A: // ↘ WHERE have they gone on their HONeymoon //
    B: // ∨↗ SOMEwhere quiet //

v) A: // ↘ WHAT's the TIME //
    B: // ∨↗ It MUST be LATE //

4.3 Listen to this example. B first agrees with something A has just said and then goes on to add some new information.

A: // ∨↗ It's imPORtant // ↘ to get it RIGHT //
B: // ↘ Of COURSE // ∨↗ it's imPORtant to get it RIGHT // ↘ but it's VERY DIFFicult //

Now, working with a partner if possible, try these. B first agrees with what A has said, using 'of course' or 'I know', and then adds some appropriate information beginning with 'but'. Try first and then listen to the recording.

i) A: // ↘ We DON'T aGREE with you //
    B: // ↘ I KNOW // ∨↗ you don't aGREE with me //
        // ↘ but   (e.g. I'm right) //

ii) A: // ↘ The ISland's BEAUtiful //
    B: // ↘   // ∨↗ it's BEAUtiful //
        // ↘ but   (e.g. too far) //

iii) A: // ↘ She likes DIamonds //
    B: // ↘   // ∨↗ she LIKES diamonds //
        // ↘ but   (e.g. expensive) //

iv) A: // ∨↗ THIS <u>HAT'S</u> // ↘ a <u>BAR</u>gain //
    B: // ↘   // ∨↗ it's a <u>BAR</u>gain //
        // ↘ but   (e.g. don't want/like/need it) //

v) A: // ↘ He's a <u>DIFF</u>icult person to <u>WORK</u> with //
   B: // ↘   // ∨↗ he's a <u>DIFF</u>icult person to <u>WORK</u> with //
       // ↘ but   (e.g. very important/clever/famous) //

4.4 Work with a partner if possible. In the first part of the reply B reminds A of things they both know, and then in the second part introduces a new idea. Listen to the example first, and then listen and repeat B's part.

A: I'm really enjoying my stay here. Where shall we go tonight?
B: We've seen all the good films, and we've been to the theatre and to a concert. Let's go to a nightclub.

Now go on in the same way. The intonation is not transcribed for you this time. Try first and then listen to the recording.

i) A: Did you get everything for the office?
    B: Here are the envelopes and the stamps. But there wasn't any paper.

ii) A: Who's coming to the dinner party?
    B: As you know, we've invited the Whites and the Robsons. But I also invited the Jenkins.

iii) A: Have we prepared everything for the party now?
    B: Well, we've organised the music and the drinks. But we haven't got the food yet.

iv) A: What have you got for the fruit salad?
    B: We've got apples and pears and peaches. We ought to get some oranges.

v) A: Where shall we go for our holiday this year?
    B: It's difficult. We've been to Italy and Greece and Austria. How do you feel about Turkey?

5 Communication activity

Student A – look at activity 6 for your information.
Student B – look at activity 9 for the information you need.

Unit 4   Revision and practice

1   Conversation

1.1 First listen to this conversation between John and Lisa and then answer the
questions.

   i)   What has Samantha told Lisa on the phone?
   ii) What is the special significance of red roses?
  iii) What are the two different meanings John and Lisa give to 'poor guy'?

1.2 In the conversation some phrases are repeated but they sound different because the speakers have chosen to highlight different words.

Listen to the first part of the conversation again as many times as you need to.

i)   Identify any phrase(s) which you hear repeated. In the transcript which follows, mark boxes round the words which you think the speaker has highlighted.

ii) Look carefully at the contexts of the phrases and try to explain why the highlighting has changed.

Lisa: That was Samantha on the phone. Honestly, I don't know how she does it.

John: Ah ... Samantha. What's she done now?

Lisa: Nothing, really. That's what's amazing. But somebody has sent her a dozen roses.

John: A dozen what?

Lisa: ... a dozen roses.

John: Roses ... mmm, I say! ... and at this time of year ...

Lisa: Yes. And a dozen roses. He must be keen.

John: Is it her birthday or something?

Lisa: No, and what's more they were red roses.

John: Now ... a dozen red roses. You know what that means.

1.3 Now listen to the second part of the conversation and do the same again.

Lisa: Yes. I know what you're going to say.

John: It means he's not just keen. He's in love with her.

Lisa: I know. I know. Poor guy ...

John: Poor guy? What do you mean? He doesn't sound very poor to me if he can afford a dozen ...

Lisa: No. I mean I feel sorry for him. He's in love with her – yes. But she's not in love with him.

John: How do you know? Did she say so?

Lisa: She doesn't even know who it is – and she says she doesn't really mind! She always ...

2 Practice activity

Listen to the following utterances which you will hear twice. Decide which of the questions, (a) or (b), provides a suitable context for what you hear.

i)   //   When we've finished LUNCH //   we'll look at the PHOtos //
     a) When can we see the photos?
     b) What shall we do after lunch?

ii) //   Your use of into<u>NA</u>tion //   can change the <u>MEAN</u>ing //
    a) What can change the meaning of what you say?
    b) Why is intonation important?

iii) //   The ho<u>TEL</u> //   was very <u>GOOD</u> //
    a) Did you enjoy your holiday?
    b) What was the accommodation like?

iv) //   You can <u>GO</u> //   if you've <u>FIN</u>ished //
    a) What shall we do now we've finished?
    b) Can we go?

Now try to say each of the utterances so that it is a suitable response to the other question.

3 Conversation

3.1 First listen to the whole of this conversation between Lisa and Tony. You heard the first part in Unit 3.

    i) What is Tony worrying about?
    ii) Do you think that Lisa feels he really needs to be worried?

3.2 Now, working with a partner if possible, listen to the second part again.

   i) Try to identify any \ and \/ tones which are not marked in the transcript below.

   ii) Try to explain why Tony and Lisa have chosen to use a \ or a \/ tone where you have marked them.

Tony: // \ I MEAN //   I MANaged to answer all the QUESTions //   and I THINK I said the right THINGS // \ but I DON'T think //   I wore the right CLOTHES //

Lisa: // \ WELL //   there's NO point in WORRYing about it // \/ what's DONE // \ is DONE //

Tony: // \ YES Lisa // \ I KNOW //   there's NOTHing I can DO about it // \ of COURSE //   I CAN'T CHANGE anything //   but I CAN'T help THINKing about it //

3.3 Now listen to the third part and do the same again.

Lisa: // \ I'm SURE // \/ you needn't WORRY //   what DID you wear // \ ANyway //

Tony: //   I HAD to put my JEANS on //

Lisa: //   Your JEANS // \ OH I SEE //

Tony: //   But I wore a TIE //

Lisa: // \/ NEver MIND //   you SAID the right things // \ ANyway //

4   Dialogue reading

Work with a partner and practise reading this dialogue. Think about which words you will highlight and where you will use \ and \/ tones. Use a \/ tone as you practised in Unit 3:

i) to refer to something that has just been stated,

ii) to check that something is as you assume,

iii) when you make a general statement which avoids answering a question.

Cathy: Hello, Bob.

Bob: Hi. You're looking well.

Cathy: Thanks. And so are you. You got back safely then?

Bob: Yes. We arrived this morning.

Cathy: This morning? I thought you were due back a couple of days ago?

Bob: Mmm, that had been the plan.

Cathy: Well, what happened?

Bob: You've heard about the rail strike?

Cathy: Oh, yes, of course. But I had forgotten you were travelling by train. How did you manage?

Bob: Well, you see, we came by coach. It took a lot longer but we got back OK.

Cathy: So I see. You don't sound as though you minded.

Bob: No. We didn't mind at all. It took a lot longer, but it was very comfortable – and it was much cheaper. In fact, we've decided to go by coach next time!

You can hear the recorded conversation, but, remember, this is only one possible version. Yours may sound different.

Unit 5   Roles and status of speakers

So far, we have identified and practised the two main tones used by speakers of English, the fall (\searrow) and the fall-rise (\vee). Another tone which you will frequently hear is the rise (\nearrow).

1   Sensitisation

1.1 Listen to this continuation of the conversation between Lisa and Tony which you heard in Units 3 and 4.

   i)   Can you hear any tones which sound more like a rise (\nearrow), rather than a fall-rise (\vee)?

   ii) If so, who uses them?

1.2 Listen again to the same part of the conversation.

i) In the transcript below the ↘ tones are marked. Try to identify the other tones as ↗ or ↘↗.

Lisa: // ↘ But ᴛᴏny //   surely you ʀᴇᴀʟised //   everybody would be wearing ꜱᴜɪᴛꜱ //   a job like ᴛʜᴀᴛ //   ꜱᴜᴄʜ a good ꜱᴀʟary //   with ꜱᴏ much responsiʙɪʟity // ↘ you ᴏᴜɢʜᴛ to have known ʙᴇᴛᴛer than to wear jeans //

Tony: // ↘ Don't reᴍɪɴᴅ me //   I ᴋɴᴏᴡ it was ꜱᴛᴜpid //

Lisa: // ↘ Well ᴡʜᴀᴛ was the ᴘʀᴏʙlem // ↘ I ᴋɴᴏᴡ //   you've ɢᴏᴛ a suit //

Tony: // ↘ Oh, ʏᴇꜱ //   I've ɢᴏᴛ one // ↘ it was at the ᴄʟᴇᴀɴer's //

Lisa: //   It was ᴡʜᴇʀᴇ //

Tony: // ↘ At the ᴄʟᴇᴀɴer's // ↘ it still ɪꜱ //

ii) If possible compare your transcript with a partner's.
iii) Try to describe the effect of the ↗ tone.

2 Explanation

In the parts of the conversation you heard in Units 3 and 4 Lisa and Tony talk to each other as equals. They are friends just exchanging information.

In the part of the conversation you have just heard in this unit Lisa becomes more assertive, as she begins to realise that Tony has, in her opinion, been silly.

She takes on a *dominant* role: you hear her refer to things she expected Tony to know or remember. When she does this she usually chooses to use a ↗ tone.

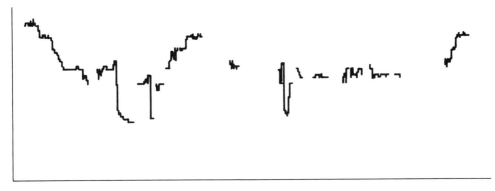

Surely you realised   everybody would be wearing suits

In some conversations the relationship between the speakers means that one of them naturally takes a dominant role. Think, for example, of a manager speaking to a worker, a doctor to a patient or a teacher to a student.

The ↗ tone is the appropriate referring tone for the dominant speaker to choose, but it would be inappropriate for the non-dominant speaker to use it.

You will see that, by choosing the ↗ tone instead of the ⌄↗ tone, speakers can exercise a sort of dominance in the conversation which may or may not be associated with their social status.

Therefore, it is important that you are able both to recognise the ↗ tone when it is used by others, and to make the correct choice between ⌄↗ and ↗ tones when you are speaking. If you use a ↗ when a ⌄↗ would have been more appropriate, you may sound self-assertive or even aggressive.

3   Imitation

3.1 Here are some of the things Lisa said to Tony. You will hear each one twice. Listen first and then repeat what Lisa says the second time you hear it.

i)   // ↗ Surely you REAlised //

ii) // ↗ SUCH a good SALary //

iii) // ↗ With so much responsiBILity //

3.2 Here are some other things Lisa said to Tony. Say them as she did and then say them using a ⌄↗. Listen first and then repeat both utterances when you have heard them the second time.

i)   // ↗ A job like THAT //
     // ⌄↗ A job like THAT //

ii) // ↗ It was WHERE //
     // ⌄↗ It was WHERE //

4   Practice activities

4.1 Listen again to this extract from the conversation. Notice that Lisa uses the ↗ tone when she responds to what Tony tells her.

Lisa: // ↘ WHAT was the PROBlem //
Tony: // ↘ It was at the CLEANer's //
Lisa: // ↗ It was WHERE //

These short dialogues are similar. In each case A chooses a ↗ tone to respond to the information B gives. Practise reading the dialogues before listening to the recording.

i)   A: // ↘ Where's FRED //
     B: // ↘ He's GONE HOME //
     A: // ↗ GONE HOME // ↘ SUREly not //
     B: // ⌄↗ He HAS //

ii) A: // ↘ How <u>OLD</u> is she //
     B: // ↘ She's THIRty-<u>FIVE</u> //
     A: // ↗ THIRty-<u>FIVE</u> // ↘ she <u>CAN'T</u> be //
     B: // ⩔ She <u>IS</u> //

iii) A: // ↘ How did you <u>GET</u> here //
     B: // ↘ I came on <u>FOOT</u> //
     A: // ↗ On <u>FOOT</u> // ↘ that's in<u>CRED</u>ible //
     B: // ⩔ I <u>DID</u> //

iv) A: // ↘ What's the <u>DATE</u> //
     B: // ↘ The TWENty-<u>FOURTH</u> //
     A: // ↗ The TWENty-<u>FOURTH</u> // ↘ <u>SURE</u>ly not //
     B: // ⩔ It <u>IS</u> //

v)   A: // ↘ How long have you <u>BEEN</u> here //
     B: // ↘ SIX <u>MONTHS</u> //
     A: // ↗ SIX <u>MONTHS</u> // ↘ I don't be<u>LIEVE</u> it //
     B: // ⩔ I <u>HAVE</u> //

4.2 Now listen again to the first dialogue from 4.1. This time the tones the speakers use in the last two lines have been changed.

A: // ↘ Where's <u>FRED</u> //
B: // ↘ He's GONE <u>HOME</u> //
A: // ⩔ GONE <u>HOME</u> // ↘ <u>SURE</u>ly not //
B: // ↗ He <u>HAS</u> //

Now B rather than A has become dominant.

Work on the dialogues which you did in 4.1 but this time use a ⩔ for A's second utterance and a ↗ for B's second utterance. Try first before listening to the recording.

4.3 Listen to this very short part of a conversation in which A has asked for directions.

B: // ↗ When you see the <u>CI</u>nema // ↘ TURN <u>LEFT</u> //
A: // ↘ <u>THANK</u> you //

When we give directions, instructions or advice we are in a dominant position. We often choose the ↗ tone for part of what we say.

Practise reading these utterances before listening to the recording.

i)   // ↗ As <u>SOON</u> as the water <u>BOILS</u> // ↘ pour it on the <u>TEA</u> //

ii) // ↗ If she <u>ASKS</u> you // ↘ <u>TELL</u> her what you <u>THINK</u> //

iii) // ↗ As you approach a <u>BEND</u> // ↘ be<u>GIN</u> to slow <u>DOWN</u> //

iv) // ↗ At the TRAffic lights // ↘ go STRAIGHT ON //

v) // ↗ WHEN you've finished THIS one // ↘ GO on to the NEXT //

The referring tone can be in the *second* half of the utterance. Listen to the example:

// ↘ TURN LEFT // ↗ when you see the CINema //

Now go on. Practise reading these utterances before listening to the recording.

i) // ↘ Go to the DENtist // ↗ if the PAIN conTINues //

ii) // ↘ Take the BATTeries OUT // ↗ if they're FINished //

iii) // ↘ Put the WARNing lights ON // ↗ if the car STOPS //

iv) // ↘ Give me a RING // ↗ when you GET to the STAtion // ↘ and I'll FETCH you //

4.4 In each of the following dialogues one of the speakers will take the dominant role. Decide which one and then, with a partner, practise reading the dialogues before listening to the recording. But remember that the recording presents only one of several possible ways of reading them.

Dialogue 1

Mrs Newell has gone to see the doctor and is discussing her problem with him.

D: Where is the pain, Mrs Newell?
Mrs N: Here, Doctor, in my chest.
D: I see. Here?
Mrs N: Yes, Doctor.
D: Does it hurt when you cough?
Mrs N: Yes, it does.
D: How long have you had it?
Mrs N: Six or seven weeks.
D: Six or seven weeks? As long as that?
Mrs N: I think so.
D: Have you tried taking anything – for the cough, I mean?
Mrs N: Well – the usual honey and hot lemon. And then I bought some cough syrup.
D: Did it help?
Mrs N: No, Doctor. That's why I've come to see you.

Dialogue 2

Jack Marsden has arranged to see his bank manager because he wants to borrow enough money to start buying a flat.

B.M.: So, you're interested in some sort of loan, Mr Marsden?

Jack: That's right. You see, I want to raise enough money for a deposit on a small flat.

B.M.: Do you mean to buy?

Jack: Yes. I don't want to go on renting.

B.M.: I see. Do you think you can get a mortgage?

Jack: Yes. I've seen about that. You see, I've got a secure job with a good salary.

B.M.: Is the flat for yourself? Will you be living there alone?

Jack: Yes. For the moment anyway. Why? Does that make any difference to the loan?

B.M.: No, no. Just interested. That's all.

Jack: Do you need to know anything else? I've brought my contract with details of my salary.

B.M.: Good. Yes, fine. And have you any securities? Shares in any companies? Insurance policies? Things like that?

5 Communication activity

> gent, well presented and willing to work hard. Salary by negotiations.– Telephone 312317
>
> REQUIRED June to August for Children's Holiday Camp in Devon: leaders for social/ sports activities. Suit responsible student with experience of work with children. Refs required. Good pay. Tel: 01–989 8989
>
> CHEMIST requires part time assistant for married and

Student A – look at activity 2 for the information you need.
Student B – look at activity 10 for your information.

Unit 6   Low Key information

As they are speaking to each other speakers sometimes lower the pitch level of their voices for some parts of what they say.

1   Sensitisation

1.1 Listen to this part of an interview and try to answer the following questions.

    i)   Why does Professor King think it is difficult to give a simple definition of 'body language'?

    ii) What examples of body language does he give?

    iii) Does he suggest that we ever use body language consciously?

1.2 Now listen to this short extract from the interview. The parts which are spoken at a low pitch level are indicated in the transcript below.

Interviewer: ... for this sixth and I'm ↓ sorry to say ↑ final programme

in the series – Professor King, who is Professor

of Psychology at Townsford University.

Thanks for coming, Professor, ↓ good of you to give us

your time. ↑ You've made a special study ...

i) In each case look carefully at what is said just before and just after the speaker lowers the pitch of his voice.

ii) There is a connection between what is said at this low pitch level and what is said immediately before or after at a 'mid' pitch level. Can you say what it is?

1.3 Now listen again to 1.1. Try to find other places where the speakers lower the pitch level of their voices.

2 Explanation

When speakers drop the pitch of their voices to this lower level we say they are using *Low Key*.

There are two common uses of Low Key:

i) The more common of the two is information which has the same meaning (more exactly, it expresses nothing which is different in meaning) as the piece of information which comes immediately before, or sometimes after, it.
e.g. '... good of you to give us your time.'
Which means the same here as 'thank you'.

ii) The second kind of Low Key information is what a speaker says as an 'aside'. In this case speakers seem to be addressing themselves rather than their hearers.
e.g. '... I'm sorry to say ...'

Speakers change the pitch of their voices to this low level on a prominent syllable:

e.g. ... sixth and I'm SORRY to SAY final ...

Professor, GOOD of you to give us your TIME. You ...

3 Imitation

Listen again to these short extracts from the conversation and repeat them. Begin at a normal or 'mid' pitch level and then drop to a low pitch level on the first prominent syllable in the second part of what you say. The arrows are there to help you.

i) ... for this sixth and I'm ↓ SORRY to SAY ↑ final programme in the series ...

ii)   Thanks for coming, Professor ↓ GOOD of you to give us your TIME. ↑

You've made a special study I understand ...

iii)   ... a subject which I ↓ KNOW I'm RIGHT in saying ↑ has a special

fascination ...

iv)   Yes, to a ↓ LARGE exTENT ↑ it is.

4   Practice activities

4.1 Listen to this short utterance and then try to say it in the same way.

We couldn't get in; there were no tickets left.

Now go on. Read these utterances and lower the pitch of your voice when you get to the part which is the same in meaning as what precedes it.

i)   Heat the oven to 400 degrees fahrenheit – that's 200 degrees centigrade.

ii)   He's studying at the University of California, in Los Angeles.

iii)   Just as I got to the station the guard blew the whistle and the train left.

iv)   Please fasten your seat belts – we're about to land.

4.2 Listen to this example:

A: Andrew's been chosen for the tennis team.
B: Has he? He's good at tennis.

Now go on. Take B's part and respond to what A says. In each case use Low Key for the part which has the same meaning as something A has said.

i)   A: Sonia's thinking of buying a Porsche.
B: Yes. She's keen on fast cars.

ii)   A: It's starting to rain.
B: Yes. They forecast wet weather.

iii)   A: He spends all his money on clothes.
B: Yes. He always wears something expensive.

iv)   A: Tony says he can't sleep at night.
B: Oh dear. He does look tired.

v)   A: Our house was built at the end of the last century.
B: Yes. I thought it was about that old.

4.3 Listen to this utterance and try to say it in the same way.

Brussels, the ↓ capital of Belgium, ↑ is the headquarters

of the Common Market.

By choosing Low Key for 'capital of Belgium' the speaker indicates that he assumes the hearer knows this fact.

Now insert some Low Key information into these sentences. Choose something you think your hearer already knows and which is not essential to your main message. You may be able to think of something yourself or you may use the ideas in the boxes.
    Then listen to the recording.

i)   In the holidays | *no lessons* / *no teachers* / *no children* | the school will be repainted.

ii) In Britain | *drive* / *on left* | the driver sits on the right.

iii) Since he gave up smoking | *doctor* / *advised* | he's been much better.

iv) In the mountains | *temperatures* / *are lower* | there could be snow.

v)   Richard Burton | *born* / *in Wales* | died in Switzerland.

4.4 First listen to this conversation between Mike and Sue. Below are some extra phrases which they could have fitted in as Low Key information. Working with a partner, first decide where suitable pieces of this information could fit. Try to think of some pieces yourself. Then practise reading the dialogue.

Mike: Sue, there you are. Have you got time for a little chat?
Sue: Of course. What is it, Mike? Is something wrong?
Mike: No, not really. But I'd like your advice.
Sue: I'll help if I can.
Mike: Well, you remember Miguel – who stayed with us last summer?
Sue: No. But I remember you telling me about him. He was very keen on sightseeing, wasn't he?
Mike: That's right. Well, I got a letter from him this morning and he's invited me to spend a holiday with his family this year. They've got a villa on Ibiza – and they've got a boat. You know how crazy I am about boats.
Sue: Mike, that's marvellous. What a wonderful opportunity for you!
Mike: Yes, but it's not that simple.

Sue: What's the problem?

Mike: It's Celia. You see, we've both been saving up like mad to go on a trip together this year.

Sue: Ah, I see. You don't want to disappoint her, of course.

Mike: That's right. She'd be so upset. She's been doing all sorts of jobs in her free time. She really deserves this holiday. It seems so unfair.

Sue: Look, Mike. First, you must tell Celia about your invitation. She'll appreciate your problem. But why don't you tell Miguel about the plans you had already made with Celia. He might even suggest ...

Low Key information

I don't	evenings and weekends
you know that	every penny we could
you look serious	she's very understanding
by going alone	I love them
very good news	wanted to go everywhere
I'm not busy	I thought you would be
naturally	

If possible record yourselves and try to decide how well you managed the Low Key parts.

There is a recording of the dialogue containing Low Key information, but remember that this is only one possible version. Yours may be quite different – particularly if you were able to think of your own Low Key pieces.

5 Communication activity

Work with a partner. You are going to tell each other a story. It can be the plot of a film, play or novel that you remember well, or something that has really happened in your life.

1 Make a list of the main events in your story.
2 Think of some Low Key pieces of information which you can include.
3 Tell your story to your partner, including the Low Key pieces. Record your stories.
4 Listen to the recording together and try to identify the Low Key pieces in your partner's story.
5 Try to suggest other Low Key pieces for your own or your partner's story and say where they could fit.

Unit 7   Contrasts

Speakers sometimes raise the pitch level of their voices for parts of what they say.

1   Sensitisation

1.1 First listen to this conversation and try to answer the questions.

   i)   Why is Tony fed up?
   ii) What seems to be his immediate problem?

1.2 Now listen again to this short extract from the beginning of the conversation.
   The parts which are spoken at a high pitch level are shown in the transcript below.

John: SO, it was ALL a huge SUCCESS?

Pat: It was fan↑TAStic!

John: Hey, ↑ LOOK. ↓ There's TONY. He LOOKS a bit fed UP.

↑ TONY. HEY, TONY.

Tony: ↑ OH, he↓LLO, JOHN. PAT! I ↑ THOUGHT you were in PARis.

Pat: Well, I ↑ WAS. I've been ↓ BACK a few DAYS now.

John: How ARE you, Tony? And HOW's your precious SPORTS car?

Tony: Don't TALK to me about it. I WISH I'd never SEEN it!

Pat: Oh, ↑ TONY. It's a LOVEly little car.

Tony: It's NOT, you know.

i) In each case look carefully at what is said immediately before and after the part spoken with raised pitch.

ii) There is a connection in meaning between what is said with raised pitch and what the speaker or someone else says in the immediate context. Can you say what the connection is?

1.3 Now listen to the rest of the conversation again and try to find other places where the speakers raise the pitch level of their voices. Mark them in the transcript below using arrows (↓ ↑) as you saw in 1.2.

Pat: But you were so PLEASED with it . . .

Tony: Oh, yes, I WAS. It was JUST what I'd DREAMED of. A BIT OLD – but in MARvellous conDITion. AND it was very CHEAP.

John: EXACTly. I reMEMber. I TOLD you at the TIME I was a bit susPICious. But you didn't LIsten.

Tony: YES, I DID. I THOUGHT I was LUCKy for once.

Pat: You WERE lucky, Tony. LAST time I saw you, you said it was so reLIable.

Tony: Well, YES. It SEEMED reLIable. For a MONTH or so. But since THEN it's been at the GARage more than on the ROAD.

John: So, WHERE is it NOW?

Tony: At the CENtral GARage. I'm HOPing to pick it UP first thing toMORRow.

John: They're exPENsive THERE.

Tony: ACTually, they're NOT. But they're not efFIcient, EIther! It was SUPPOSED to be ready on MONday.

Pat: MONday! But tomorrow's THURSday. COME ON, CHEER UP, Tony. You'll HAVE it for the weekEND.

Tony: Not necessARily. Every time I GO or RING they've found something ELSE that needs DOing. LAST weekend was bad eNOUGH without it. But THIS weekend is REALly important. SaMANtha said ...

2 Explanation

When speakers raise the pitch of their voices to a high level they do so on a prominent syllable and we say they are using *High Key*. They use High Key to express things they consider to be contrary to what their hearers expect. These things contrast with something which has already been said or implied, or with something which is implicit in the context.

There are three kinds of contrast we often hear:

i) Word/idea contrast

   e.g. But you were so PLEASED with it ...

ii) Disagreement

   e.g. Yes, I DID.

iii) Strong agreement

   e.g. It was fanTAStic.

NOTE

(i) and (ii) are more clearly contrastive than (iii). Strong agreement is a contrast of a different kind. Although there is agreement, there is disagreement with the way something has been expressed and then the same idea is expressed in a contrastive/stronger way.

3   Imitation

Listen to these short extracts from the conversation and, in each case, repeat only the second speaker's part.

i)   John: But you didn't listen.

    Tony: Yes, I ↑ DID.

ii)   John: They're expensive there.

    Tony: ↑ ACTually, they're ↓ NOT.

iii)   Tony: I thought I was lucky for once.

    Pat: You ↑ WERE lucky, Tony.

iv)   John: So, it was all a huge success?

    Pat: It was fan↑TAStic!

4   Practice activities

4.1   For this activity work with a partner if possible. For each of A's utterances there are two responses for B. Choose the one which would be spoken in High Key.

i)   A: So, you couldn't do it?
    B: a) No, even though I tried and tried.
        b) Yes. I managed it in the end.

ii)   A: She's made her decision then?
    B: a) No. She still doesn't know what to do.
        b) Yes, she has.

iii)   A: I enjoy horror films.
    B: a) So do I.
        b) I hate them.

iv)   A: Do you remember – you ate oysters?
    B: a) I never eat oysters.
        b) Yes – I think I remember.

v)   A: I think we should go by plane.
    B: a) We can't. It's too expensive.
        b) I think so too.

4.2 First listen to this short utterance and try to say it in the same way. The High Key is not marked for you.

The journey was all right, but the hotel was awful.

Now go on. Read these utterances and raise the pitch level of your voice when you get to the part which contrasts with what has been said (or with what the speaker thinks the hearer expects).

i)   I asked him to help me but he wouldn't.

ii) Roger managed to solve one problem but created another.

iii) We telephoned for an ambulance and they sent a fire engine.

iv) We expected the results to be bad, but they were terrible.

4.3 The pictures represent information which you should say in High Key. Work with a partner if possible and decide which utterance, (a) or (b), can be completed with it. Practise reading both utterances.
      Then listen to the recording, which contains High Key.

i)   a) She's been saving all her money because she ...
     b) She went to buy a bicycle and came back with ...

ii) a) He wanted to work in the library ...
     b) It was very late when he went to the library ...

iii) a) He went to an Indian restaurant and ordered ...
     b) He went to the fast food place and ordered ...

iv) a) The little boys wanted ...
     b) The old ladies wanted ...

v) a) He needs to lose weight and ...
    b) He loves sweet things ...

4.4 First read this conversation. Then work with a partner and study it, one
section at a time, to decide where the speakers would use High Key. Then
practise reading it.

Section 1

A: So, I hope you're packed and ready to leave.
B: Yes, yes. I'm packed but not quite ready. I can't find my passport.
A: Your passport? That's the one thing you mustn't leave behind.
B: I know. I haven't lost it. I've packed it and I can't remember which bag
    it's in. Oh dear.
A: Well, you'll have to find it at the airport. Come on.

Section 2

A: Come on. The taxi's waiting.
B: Did you say taxi? I thought we were going in your car.
A: Yes, well, I had planned to. But I'll explain later. You've got to be there
    in an hour.
B: Not an hour. The plane doesn't leave for two hours. Anyway, I'm ready
    now. We can go.
A: Now – you're taking just one case. Is that right?
B: No, there's one in the hall as well.
A: Gosh! What a lot of stuff! You're taking enough for a month, instead of
    a week.
B: Well, you can't depend on the weather. It might be cold.
A: It's never cold in Tenerife. Certainly not in May. Come on. We really
    must go.

Section 3

B: Right. We're ready. We've got the bags. I'm sure there's no need to rush.
A: There is. I asked the taxi driver to wait two minutes – not twenty.
B: Look, I'm supposed to be going away to relax. You're making me
    nervous.
A: Well, I want you to relax on holiday. But you can't relax yet.
B: OK, OK, I promise not to relax! At least not until we get to the airport

and I find my passport. Then there will be something else to worry about
  I suppose.
A: Maybe not for you. But I don't know how I'm going to get back.

If possible, record yourselves and try to decide how well you managed.
  There is a recording of the dialogue, but remember that it is only one of
several possible versions.

5 Communication activity

Student A – look at activity 3 for the information you need.
Student B – look at activity 7 for your information.

Unit 8   Revision and practice

1   Conversation

1.1 Listen to the whole of the continuation of the conversation between Tony and Lisa which you heard in Unit 5.

Can you describe the ways in which Tony's plans went wrong?

1.2 Now listen again to the part you have not heard before.

    i)   In the transcript below the ↘ tones are marked but the ↘︎ and the ↗ tones are not. Try to identify these two tones and mark them in the transcript.

Lisa: // ↘ You're HOPEless //   here you ARE //   with the CHANCE of a LIFEtime //   to get exACTly the job you WANT //   you have ALL the right qualifiCAtions //   a LOT of exPERIence //   NO family TIES //   and when the DAY of the interview aRRIVES //   YOU'RE in the INterview room //↘ and your SUIT's in the CLEANer's //

Tony: // ↘ I KNOW // ↘ I KNOW //

Lisa: // ↘ WELL // ↘ WHAT HAppened //   did you forGET to GO for it //   lose your TICKet // ↘ or WHAT //

Tony: // ↘ NO //   but I ASKED SaMANtha // ↘ to pick it UP for me // ↘ and they GAVE her the wrong ONE //   by the time I got BACK to the SHOP // ↘ it was CLOSED //

ii) Discuss your transcript with someone else.

2 Practice activities

2.1 When Lisa becomes assertive and tells Tony, 'You ought to have known better than to wear jeans', Tony accepts her criticism. If he had reacted more strongly against her and tried to be more dominant, he would probably have chosen to use ↗ tones where he used ∨↗ tones.

Transcribed below is part of the conversation but this time Tony uses ↗ tones where you heard him use ∨↗ tones.

Work with a partner and practise reading the dialogue in this way. If possible record yourselves and compare it with the original.

Lisa: You ought to have known better than to wear jeans.
Tony: // ↗ Don't reMIND me // ↗ I KNOW it was STUpid //
Lisa: Well, what was the problem? I know you've got a suit.
Tony: // ↗ Oh, YES // ↗ I've GOT one // ↘ it was at the CLEANer's //

2.2 If Lisa had been less self-assertive in her conversation with Tony, she would have chosen the ∨↗ tone where you heard her use the ↗ tone.

Transcribed below is part of the conversation, but this time Lisa uses ∨↗ tones. Try reading what Lisa says in this way and, if possible, record yourself. Then you can compare this version with the way Lisa spoke in the conversation.

Lisa: // ↘ You're HOPEless // ∨↗ here you ARE // ∨↗ with the CHANCE of a LIFEtime // ∨↗ to get exACTly the job you WANT // ∨↗ you have ALL the right qualifiCAtions // ∨↗ a LOT of exPERIence // ∨↗ NO family TIES // ∨↗ and when the DAY of the interview aRRIVES // ↘ YOU'RE in the INterview room // ↘ and your SUIT's in the CLEANer's //

3   Conversation

3.1 First listen to this conversation and try to answer the questions.

  i) Where has Pat been and why?
  ii) What has she brought back?

3.2 In this conversation Lisa and Pat sometimes drop the pitch of their voices to a low level for parts of what they say. They use Low Key.

  Listen to the first part of the conversation again and in the transcript below use arrows (↓ and ↑) to mark off the parts you think are in Low Key. Each one begins with a word containing a prominent syllable.

Section 1

Lisa: It WON'T be long before we're BACK, Pat; there's NOT much on the ROAD. HOW ARE you ANYWAY?

Pat: FINE, THANKS. NOW the FLIGHT's over. It's REALLY GOOD of you to come out SO LATE, Lisa. I'm SORRY you had to wait SO LONG; you MUST have been here an HOUR.

Lisa: DON'T WORRY. It WASN'T YOUR fault. ANYWAY, I BROUGHT a good BOOK. I always DO, in CASE there's a deLAY. We KNEW the plane had LEFT late. They MADE an anNOUNCEment.

  i) Compare your transcript with a partner.
  ii) Look at the parts you have marked as Low Key and together decide how each one relates to what has been said just before.

3.3 Now listen to the other two sections and do the same again.

Section 2

Pat: WELL, I'm so glad you DID come. There AREn't any TRAINS now – NOT at THIS hour.

Lisa: I'm REAlly looking FORward to HEARing about your TRIP. It seems AGEs since you WENT. WHEN WAS it?

Pat: ONly a couple of WEEKS ago. At the beGINNing of the MONTH. But I aGREE – it DOES seem ages. But I've DONE such a LOT in that time, met SO many PEOple ...

Lisa: Was it ALL business, or DID you find time for PLEAsure?

Pat: I spent MOST of the time WORKing – well, every MORNing and afterNOON.

Section 3

Lisa: You DIDn't get the CHANCE to go to any GALLeries or muSEums – WORKing every DAY.

Pat: NO, I DIDn't. Not THIS time. But it WAS a BUSiness trip; I DIDn't exPECT to. I was VISiting the big FASHion houses and THAT sort of thing, which I CAN'T do in LONdon.

Lisa: It sounds SO exCIting – you ARE LUCky. Did you BUY anything? I'd LOVE to SEE what's in those SUITcases.

Pat: I THINK you MIGHT be disappOINted, Lisa. NO deSIGNer clothes, you know. JUST a few CHEAP things that TOOK my EYE.

4 Practice activities

4.1 First listen to each of the recorded utterances. Then, for each one decide which of the two statements, (a) or (b), best explains the meaning.

   i) a) We didn't know how she would respond.
       b) We expected her to accept.

   ii) a) They've never been anywhere exciting before.
        b) You're interested to know where they've gone, so I'm telling you.

  iii) a) I've never heard of it snowing in the south before.
        b) The weather was the same in the south as the north – it snowed.

  iv) a) She didn't come alone.
        b) We expected her to come alone.

   v) a) She shouldn't have washed it in the washing machine.
        b) The shirt is normally washed in the machine.

4.2 First listen to each of the recorded utterances. Then, for each one decide which of the two statements, (a) or (b), best explains the meaning.

    i) a) I knew he'd get the job.
       b) I wasn't sure he'd get the job – but he did.

   ii) a) Some of the instructions are important – just read these.
        b) All the instructions are important – read them all.

  iii) a) They could have gone in a number of ways.
        b) There is no other way to do the rest of the journey.

  iv) a) Her friends can skate and she wants to learn to skate too.
        b) She wants to learn to skate in the same way as her friends.

   v) a) There are several doctors there and he is speaking to the one who has just arrived.
        b) There is one doctor there and he/she has just arrived.

4.3 For this activity take B's part and respond to the recording, or work in pairs. In each case, B should choose the response, (a) or (b), which contains information to be presented in Low Key.

    i) A: Where did he go?
       B: a) He went to the greengrocer's to buy some potatoes.
           b) He went to the umbrella shop to buy an umbrella.

   ii) A: What do you want to see when you travel?
       B: a) I want to see the pyramids in Egypt.
           b) I want to see some castles in Germany.

  iii) A: What's he going to do on holiday?
       B: a) He took his racket so he could play squash.
           b) He took his skis so he could do some skiing.

  iv) A: When will you come back?
       B: a) Sometime in the summer when it's warmer.
           b) Sometime in the summer when they give me permission.

Communication activities

1

You are a customer in a small restaurant and are ready to order. The menu is quite limited, but there are different kinds/flavours of each thing.

Student B is the waiter/waitress and will ask you for your order.

1 Choose from the menu what you would like for each course.
2 Ask the waiter/waitress for more information.
3 Choose from the selection of things you are offered.

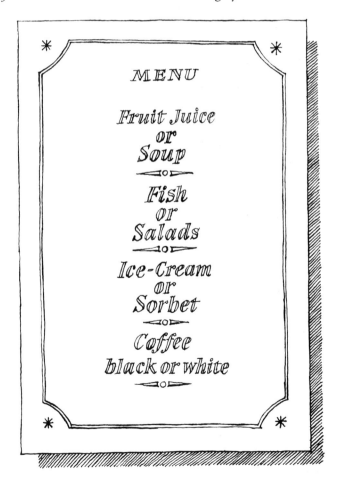

MENU

Fruit Juice
or
Soup

Fish
or
Salads

Ice-Cream
or
Sorbet

Coffee
black or white

2

You are the Director of the Children's Holiday Camp which has advertised for leaders.

Student B is interested in the advertisement and telephones you. Try to find out if he/she would be suitable by asking questions. He/she will ask you for further information.

JOB DESCRIPTION

JOB   To supervise children aged 10–16

DATES   June 1st to August 31st (leaders must work
             as many weeks as possible, mininimum 4
             weeks)

HOURS   7am to 9pm, 6 days a week

DUTIES   To organise day/evening activities, to
             supervise children at night

QUALITIES 1 Physically <u>fit</u>; age 18–26
           2 Able to <u>organise sports</u> – swimming,
              sailing, windsurfing, hiking, climbing,
              ball games, etc.
           3 <u>Sociable</u>; must organise parties, discos,
              barbecues, competitions, campfire sing-
              songs, etc.
           4 <u>Responsible</u> and able to understand/
              control children; preferably with
              experience
           5 Simple <u>medical knowledge</u>

           <u>PAY</u> £90 per week, including accommodation
           and meals

If you think student B might be suitable, make an appointment to meet him/her next Friday at 101 Cambridge Street.

3

You have just come back from holiday in Spain *or* France. You meet student B who you know has been on holiday in Morocco *or* Italy.

Ask your friend about his/her holiday — assuming he/she did the same sort of things as you.
e.g. You stayed in a hotel, so ask about student B's hotel.
     You travelled by air, so ask what his/her flight was like.

Using the information below, *answer* B's questions about your holiday. *Do not offer* information until you are asked about that part of the holiday.

Information

```
You travelled by air - It was a charter flight and was
  crowded and uncomfortable.
Your holiday lasted two weeks - You got home yesterday.
You stayed in a big hotel - It was new and hadn't much
  character.
The hotel was near the beach - You spent all your time
  sunbathing and swimming.
You didn't do any sightseeing - In fact, you didn't travel at
  all while you were there.
You didn't eat any local/traditional food - The hotel gave
  you 'international tourist' food.
You enjoyed a really good night life - varied and exciting.
NOW - You have no money left.
```

4

You work in the Tourist Information office in Tonbridge, a town in south-east England. Student B is staying in Tonbridge for a few days and wants to visit the interesting places in the area.

He/she will bring a map and ask you:
i) for information about some towns and cities.
ii) where certain things can be found.

INFORMATION SHEET

BODIAM — A large medieval castle.

BRIGHTON — A seaside town with many holiday attractions.

CANTERBURY — Ancient walled city with magnificent cathedral and many historic buildings. Nearby is a zoo.

HASTINGS — Holiday town and fishing port. A ruined castle and smugglers' caves.

HEVER — A lovely village with large castle which was once owned by King Henry VIII. Beautiful gardens.

LULLINGSTONE — Remains of fine Roman villa with baths and mosaic floors.

ROCHESTER — Historic city with cathedral and Norman castle. Charles Dickens wrote here — Dickens Centre.

RYE — Pretty old town. Many artists live here.

5

You are a waiter/waitress in a small restaurant. The customer's menu is limited and student A will need more information about the kinds/flavours of the things in each course before he/she can order.

1 Ask the customer to choose something for the first course.
2 Give more information about the thing he/she chooses.
3 Then ask about the next course.

Menu

Friday 13th

Starters
Fruit juice — pineapple, grapefruit, orange
Soup   — tomato, vegetable, mushroom

Main course
Fish   — cod, trout, plaice
Salads   — chicken, salmon, egg, cheese

Dessert
Ice-cream   — vanilla, chocolate, strawberry
Sorbet   — lemon, peach, raspberry

Coffee   — black or white

6

1 Working with your partner think of all the things you both do together, e.g. school lessons, evening classes, etc. and write them in your diaries for next week.

2 Now, working individually, write down in your diary the appointments you have next week or activities that your partner doesn't know about.

	Morning	Afternoon	Evening
SUN			
MON			
TUE			
WED			
THUR			
FRI			
SAT			

3 Try to arrange to meet:
   i) for coffee.
   ii) to see a film together.

7

You have been on holiday in Morocco *or* Italy. You meet student A who you know has been on holiday in Spain *or* France.

Ask your friend about his/her holiday – assuming he/she did the same sort of things as you.
e.g. You did part of the journey by boat, so ask him/her if the sea was calm.
     You visited lots of interesting places, so ask student A about the places he/she
         visited.

Using the information below, *answer* A's questions about your holiday. *Do not offer* information until you are asked about that part of your holiday.

Information

You made the journey by boat and train - and took your
    bicycle.
You were away for three weeks - arrived back last week.
You camped in a small tent which you took with you.
You stayed in a different place every night - always
    somewhere quiet.
You spent all your time visiting places of historical
    interest - your special interest is art.
You ate good country food - enjoyed the regional
    specialities.
You were not at all interested in any night life - You spent
    the evenings reading about the places you planned to visit.
NOW you feel fit and healthy - You spent very little, so you
    have a lot of money left.

8

You are staying in Tonbridge for a few days and have gone to the Tourist Information office. Student A works there and is going to help you. You have taken this map, where you have marked a few places, and some notes about things you would like to see.

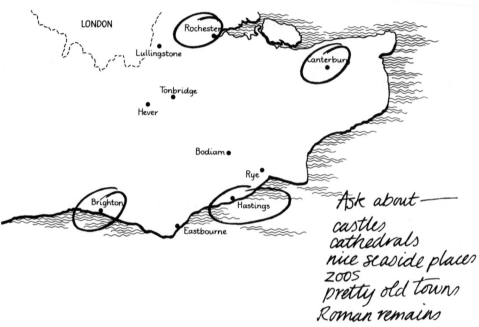

Ask:
i)   for information about the places you have marked.
ii) where you can find the things you would like to see.

9

1 Working with your partner think of all the things you both do together, e.g. school lessons, evening classes, etc. and write them in your diaries for next week.

2 Now, working individually, write down in your diary the appointments you have next week or activities that your partner doesn't know about.

	Morning	*Afternoon*	*Evening*
SUN			
MON			
TUE			
WED			
THUR			
FRI			
SAT			

3 Try to arrange to meet:
   i) for coffee.
   ii) to see a film together.

10

You are a student who has seen the advertisement for leaders at a Children's Holiday Camp.

It interests you and so you telephone. Student A is the Director of the camp, who answers the phone. Answer his/her questions and ask for further information.

PERSONAL INFORMATION

AGE — 20

OCCUPATION — Student of Biological Science at London University

PAY — £80 per week minimum

DATES — 20 June to 31 August

EXPERIENCE —
i) Have organised visits and social evenings for foreign students on holiday courses
ii) Have six younger brothers and sisters; used to baby-sitting

SPORTS — Basketball, tennis, table tennis, all water sports

INTERESTS — Belong to a Nature Society; keen on hill walking and rock climbing
Can play the guitar and sing
Enjoy social events

QUALIFICATIONS — Swimming/life-saving certificate
Driving licence
Elementary First Aid Certificate

REFERENCES — Can supply good references

EXTRA INFORMATION You want a holiday job where you can earn a lot of money because you want to visit the USA in September. You want to know about free time. You would like at least one full day free.

You may be asked for an interview so you must decide whether or not you want to be considered for the job by the end of the call.

Glossary

UTTERANCE

In normal conversation we do not always speak in full sentences nor in single sentences. *Utterance* means any piece of conversation which may, but will not always, correspond to a sentence.

PROMINENCE

In any utterance at least one word will seem more noticeable than the others. Such a word contains a *prominent* syllable. This is shown in the transcription by the use of small capital letters.

PITCH

We use the word *pitch* to describe the **high** or **low** sound of the voice. It does not refer to loud, soft, fast or slow. Every individual has a level of pitch which is normal, and which we can recognise as his/her middle pitch level. He/she can change it to make the voice **high** or **low** in relation to this middle level.

TONE

Tone is used to describe a change in the direction in the pitch movement of a speaker's voice, which takes place as a single glide, e.g. a fall ($\searrow$) or a rise ($\nearrow$). A speaker chooses a particular tone, from a small number of possibilities, according to the way he/she wishes to present his/her message.

TONIC SYLLABLE

A speaker begins the pitch movement we have called *tone* on a prominent syllable. This syllable is then called a *tonic syllable* and is indicated in the transcriptions by the use of small capital letters and underlining.

TONE UNIT

A *tone unit* is an utterance or part of an utterance which contains a single tone and, therefore, one tonic syllable. A speaker may make one or two (not usually more) syllables in a tone unit prominent. The same piece of speech can be divided into a different number of tone units, depending on how many tones the speaker chooses to use. The beginnings and endings of tone units are indicated in the transcription by the use of two slanting lines (//).

KEY

Speakers may move directly up ↑ or down ↓ from their middle pitch level for parts of what they say. We call this variation between pitch levels for parts of what is said *key*. There are, of course, differences in the middle pitch level of individuals, but for every speaker we can hear the three levels, which we call Mid, High and Low Key. The move up or down in the level of pitch is quite separate and independent from the gliding movement of pitch which we call *tone*.